Jane Philips Meneghini
Khotso Publishing, 2024
ISBN 978-1-7375868-7-6

Singing Over the Bones

by

Jane Philips Meneghini

*"Then we must sit by the fire and think about
which song we will use to
sing over the bones,
which creation hymn, which re-creation hymn."*

--Lydia Pinkola Estes

For my parents,
Fletcher R. Philips (1908-1970)
and Lucille Hansen Philips (1908-2004)

INVOCATION

Sister sublime, robed in mists
            you sit in my small craft
            wordless, though you know the way

You compel me to row through fog and night
            lost circles in lapping shadows.

I call you Lady Solitude
            of the long hands and motionless feet.

Once you demanded sacrifice. You stood by my
shoulder
       still as a pillar, your colorless veils   fluting,
       and watched me make the potion of love and
death.

You are she who prevails by silences.

I must row through the swamp of dreams
            where true outlines
            drift and bend like mist around us.

Come with me again.
Watch and say nothing.
It is up to me to save us both.

--JM

CONTENTS
Singing Over the Bones

Singing
Over
the
Bones

BEGINNING
July 1938

Lucille lay in the mahogany bed of her happiness with one tanned leg resting across the thigh of her sleeping husband and stared into the hot, breathless pre-dawn darkness, waiting for another pain. When it came, sharp as knives in her lower belly, she bit her lip and drew in breath as she counted. Her mother and Dr. Swan seemed to be in her head, as close to her now as her husband seemed far away. Three, four, five . . .*count the length of contractions and the time between them*, said Dr. Swan, unruffled, cool and pin-striped. *Childbearing is the hardest of woman's woes*, her mother said, wiping her hands on her apron as if she'd interrupted kneading her bread to come and help. Twenty five, twenty-six, twenty-seven… The contraction melted away. Lucille eased cautiously onto her side and wrapped her arm around her husband's back, giving him a hug with the baby between them. He didn't stir. He would be so excited. But she let him sleep until the first rosy light gleamed around the edges of the shade, and their new day began.

THE END OF WINTER

The tides of snow that come in March linger,
  froth of winter
sinking slowly into earth's dark riffles,
  its hummocks and burrows.

Today the road to Hancock village turned
  to brown-sugar beneath my boots.
A truck slithered down a mud-slick hill.
  Blackbirds called from reed to reed

Late in the night while wind blows
  round the house, I read:

> *...at this time of year Indians dug*
> *for roots and buds; wolves, vermin*
> *large and small got at stored food.*
> *Wolverines, demoniac*
> *with infernal ancestry , stole meat from traps,*
> *leaving a bloody mess....*

Still the slip-silver moon rises
  over the hills.
Tell me a story, mother, with *infernal,*
  silver and *slither* in it.

Tell of the man you loved once
    for his liquid clarinet,
his sad past and cruel mother. You,
    link to my link, once single,

chaste of soul and eager, tell me your love
    had nothing dark in it.
Outside the sky turns diffuse and pale
    barred with the black limbs of oaks.
                    --JM   Oct. 12, 2020

A Story: What Happened? You Did.
Mother and Daughter Sit with the Photo Album

You were always your father's daughter.
Apple of his eye. The bee's knees.

Before you came, no one could have asked
for a more loving husband than I had.

Then you were born and he just stopped.
Wanting. It was as if you were enough

to satisfy the longing he had, without
even knowing it, for something perfect.

When he came in the door every night, he'd
pick you up, carry you to the living room.

He fed you, sang to you. I'd hear you two
laughing as I finished making dinner.

It was never the three of us. You and he,
a twosome, right from the beginning.

Here, I want you to keep this picture. See
how young we were. It was Christmas Eve.

I was carrying you. We both wanted you
so much. We were waiting. Together.

PARTNERS

The whirring voice in the cloud turned
my mother faster   faster
she danced round
the blackberry bush   a beaten
time ago forlorn
and gone again.
she cooked and cleaned
hung out the wash
"I know why you've gotten fat," the neighbor
Leered and leaned. My mother
fled. she slammed the door she whirled against the china
cupboard. "Your a cow in a crystal shop," my mother said.
"And a horse in the kitchen," too.

GRANDMOTHER
--for Anastasia McGurney Hansen

An Irish farmer's youngest girl, you were
his highest hope until he died. Your mother
ran a boarding house, then seemed to disappear.

Ellie the eldest took you in and all
your sisters called you handsome. Gentile
milliner by trade, maker of hats with veils
and feathers, you tumbled and fell
for a tall Norwegian carpenter
who drove a hook-and-ladder.

You ruled our apartment building with quiet
Victorian policy, a queen on Colfax Ave.
while your careful daughters tiptoed around.

In old brown pictures you stand
still erect, your hand on a chair,
mouth a small prim curve, head
crowned with Gibson Girl hair.
Staunch in your starched white
shirtwaist and leg o'mutton sleeves,
a long heavy skirt pulled tight
over firm, corseted hips.

But I knew your lap's soft hills,
your apron's sprawl of flowers,
yielding warmth by my cheek,
the dangling brooch from China,
your scent of blossoms and yeast,
stories you laughed as you told,
the gentle sway of the rocker
long before we grew old.
rev. Jan. 2021

Anastasia McGurney was the youngest child of Irish immigrants Margaret Brian and Peter McGurney. She was born in 1881 in Campus, Illinois.

CLARINET POLKA

Dad's long fingers lifted the licorice stick
from its velvet nest, fitted the pale reed
to the black mouth piece, licked it twice,
tucked his lips--
then his fingers flew along silver keys.
Round-armed Marybelle pushed and pulled
her squeeze box
nodding her curls in time.
Red-faced Al collapsed on sofa pillows,
puffing cigar smoke notes above his head.
The tall man with the sax
tooted and honked,
his humming wife clapped along.
My mother in her flowered dress
played so fast and frolicking
she forgot me there
under the lilting piano
my heart filling up with song.

FORTE

Power pounded from mother's piano
entering me as I sat beneath.
I watched her feet march the pedals,
her hands, they shook the air around.

Tumult set my body ringing,
clamor filled my bones, chords more
felt than heard, glissandos shivered
along my spine into my trilling head.

Chopin strode across the room
molto agitato and Polonaise Militaire.
She thundered through her Liszt recital,
began Rachmaninov, stumbled, stopped.

Started, stumbled. As if her fingers
refused to scale those octaves, finished.
Sat a while, closing pages, then left the room.
I remained behind, listening to silence.

THE WAR ON COLFAX AVENUE

In a small apartment on south side Chicago,
five rooms are dark except where my mother sits
in her bedroom, nursing, rocking my sister slow.

One dim lamp on her dresser makes a glow
where we three are enclosed, windows blinded,
doors all shut. Outside, father patrols

the block. I saw him go in his khaki coat,
a red cross on his helmet. He carries a stick
to guard the neighborhood, mother says, sees

the blackout's kept until the sirens sound.
I may turn out the light and peek through
the blind into the city night. All blackness

out there. No street lamp or car. Not even a moon.
My father might be walking past the mountain
of flattened tin cans in the empty lot or stopping

at the first aid station in the basement below
where Butchie lives, cots standing in rows,
bandages in piles. I dreamt about that once.

I lower the blind with care and grope for my mother.
The baby makes soft sounds. Mother's arm is warm
where I lean against her. Her warmth seems to grow,

wrapping me, the baby, the whole room in a dark glow
as the low drone of practice bombers begins in the west
becoming slowly a roar that shakes the air over our heads.

2008

BEING 4-*F*

The day my father went to war
wearing his fedora and overcoat
mother spent the morning primping.
On that day I did not watch
her spritzing violets
as she sat before her mirror
in a silver slip, her hair bright
damp tendrils from the shower.
I did not sort through her jewelry box
asking for stories of Joe
who gave the jade heart and crystal beads,
who took her dancing before he died
in the days of flappers and speakeasies.
Not on the day when my father went
to the draft. "Watch for him," she said.

I waited at the window on my little red chair.
When he came striding
from the 79th Street Car, I cried,
"He's coming! He's here!"
She ran to meet him at the door.
They stood in the hall embracing
and kissing. Kissing, and I
hugged their legs. For a while
We filled that somber place
with something as bright as crystal.

SALVAGE

Everyone salvaged cans and bacon fat for the War.
Grandma salvaged sheets simply to be clever.

She ripped double sheets down worn middles,
sewed unworn selvages together, making sturdy

seams toenails would not rip while dreaming.
Not sheets for honeymooners but good for years

of passing through the wringer like flattened
tongues snaking down into the cold deep

blue-tinged laundry waters, then freed to flap
above the lawn. The women gathered them

before dinner-- fragrant, sun-warmed armloads.
These are the sheets of childhood, where I lay

a little left of center, like a princess
avoiding a pea, stretched out legs that ached

from too much running, buried my face
in summer and fell into unconsciousness with ease.

BEFORE BREAKFAST

Tug, tug, tug,
the rhythmic pull
of my mother's hands
braiding my thick, straight hair.

Sit still.

It's hot outside and bright, dim in the room my sister
shares with me. Light seeps through the sooty screen.

Tug, tug, tug
snap of the rubber band.
Sit still.
There's the other side
to do.
Then get off the stool.

Mother lifts my sister up,
begins to brush her tangled mop.

She always cries, I say with disgust.
Because it hurts, my mother says.

She holds a hank of snarls,
yanks the comb right through.
A tooth snaps off and flies.
Ow! my sister wails.

Honey, I'm almost through.

Around two fingers my mother wraps
my sister's hair with the comb.
Banana curls fall to her shoulders
in shining rows, like Shirley Temple's
do. Mother adds a yellow bow.

I'm hungry! I whine and fret.
Years pass before I call it envy.

GRANDFATHER
FOR CHRISTIAN HANSEN--1

I don't know what came first in the way
you live in my mind
still on Colfax Ave, that brick three-flat
bought in the Depression with a fireman's pay

for a song, mother said. The tune of it
plays round in my head, a whole symphony
in the city between two vacant lots
where you made things grow--

from waste land and a handful of seeds
came green-leaf towers hung with beefsteak tomatoes,
frill-topped of carrots in straight stony rows
where their roots grew crooked and sweet,

radishes bulging red and white above the dirt
among long veridian wands of scallion tops,
chartreuse lettuce ruffling next to the dark
spade-leafed spinach, before everything

bolted under Chicago's hot June sky.
On the dry slope shouldering the fence
you set out spindly shoots from the cold frame
while I peppered you with skeptical questions.

The only reply I remember
tumbled downhill, an astonishment of brightness--

hundred-colored moss roses delicate and tough
singing in the stony soil.

FOR CHRISTIAN HANSEN—2
The Maker's Place

In your basement precinct, the "bathroom" was
like a clue. Chicago Yellow Pages dangled
from an overhead pipe, providing
toilet paper along with plenty
to read. At the sink, scrubbed to dullness,
speckled with a confetti
of paint, soap was gritty and came from a can
like the ones in gas stations. Gas station ambiance
before minimarts.

Your workshop windows looked out
through cobwebs onto ankles of passers-by
headed for the 79th Streetcar. The workbench,
how to tell it, its surface pocked and slicked
with uneven layers of dried paint and shellac,
dented by battering hammers intent
on their projects. Around us light seemed dim
except for the brilliant circle a goose-necked lamp
shone on your hands--your sandpaper fingers
sliding shallow drawers out and in, out and in,
choosing among pattern-makers' tools delicate
as a dentist's gleaming in green velvet grooves.

If I didn't talk you let me stay
with you among the shelves of paint cans
arrangements of saws, chisels, screw-drivers, rasps
glass jars of screws, nails, bolts, washers.
Around us the air smelled of sawdust and turpentine.
And something else salty and old.

Over our heads my mother's feet went back and forth
between table, refrigerator, pantry and stove.
Over her head my grandmother's feet the same
pattern.
It was you I wanted to be like.

You taught me to fish, stabbing
the twisting worm in three places

pulling the barb through, leaving worm-ends
free to writhe. Your big square hands

creased with ground-in dirt, coal-dust and oil
tied deft knots in leader and line. I still

hear your voice, a gruff man teaching--
 "It doesn't hurt. It's just a worm so stop crying."

Red and white ball bobbing on pea green pond--
"That's your fish. Pull back. Set the hook!"

The line quickens, grows taut. A thrill
courses through bamboo

into hands, bones, nerves. Facing
the caught fish, its terrified stare,

working, blood-stained mouth, sucking gills
my hand around its mucous-slick flanks

unhooking the hook, tossing the fish back in,
its glad plop, quick-silver flash away--

I would murder worms for this.
And that mysterious shock of touching
something wild.

FOR CHRISTIAN HANSEN—4

The last time I saw you, you clambered
between parallel bars, learning to walk

again, your legs more bowed than ever
a grin on your face like a kid's

showing off for your great-grandsons
while the physical therapist told

how hard you worked
            a game old man.

You died in a bed with high sides
like a child's crib, far from me.

I imagine your wrists tethered
by soft straps. You were hooked

to lines and pierced by needles

You still managed to slip quick
                away in the night
                    the way you planned.

PA - August. 1937.

Chris was the oldest of seven boys and one girl who died as an infant. I was told Maria Hansen never got over her death.

Maria and Peter Hansen

HEARTS

The crooked green heart hung on her crystal and jade necklace,
one edge angled off sharply where it should have curved out.
I stood beside her dressing table tracing the twisting pattern
carved across its surface, asking for stories about Joe

who gave her jewelry every Christmas, who drove her
in his yellow roadster to speak-easies in the Loop, who once
escaped a raid with her, like Bonnie and Clyde. Joe died
of consumption, finally. *Why didn't you marry him?*

Oh, honey, he wouldn't have made a good husband.
Her theories of marriage mingled with spritzes
of perfume, pink glow of powder and rouge,
light-hearted hope that father would respond to primping.

What did Daddy give you?
She wriggled the fingers
of her diamond hand and sparkled with mischief.

We grew apart, my mother and I, but she remembered.
She gave me her jade necklace a few years before she died.
The chain is tarnished, she said.
I took it with a smile and kiss for the memory of her
sitting at her dressing table in the rosy light,
my soft, round, curly-haired
Momma with a past.

WINTER WEEK DAYS

"These are the suburbs of acquiescence..."
from <u>An Atlas of the Difficult World</u> by Adrienne Rich

On the city-edge of non-complaint
the accountant leaves the first-floor flat
and walks to the I. C. station cold mornings,
his heels counting pavement between grim drifts
with the leather thud of custom wingtips,
his feet long and narrow,
beyond ordinary feet.

On his cheek he bears the cool kisses
of his wife's lips, milk and sugar
planted twice, his own lips pecking the air
near her face and his children watching
eyes round over their bowls,
Gordon MacRae on the radio singing
oh what a beautiful, beautiful day.

He returns in darkness on the 5:45 express,
his brief case a burden in his hand, brown fedora
low on his balding head, scarf a dash of red,
trench-tan rain coat over tired three-piece suit,
wool dark as coal in the basement bin.
But he thinks of the set table, the table shining,

and his daughters' faces laughing.
He rehearses to his measured steps
a story to tell called Day at the Office,
while his wife clears plates and serves
almond tarts from the bakery, or éclairs.
Night will grow cold and black outside.
Inside, the small glow of evensong.

TALE OF THE ANKLE-GRABBER

When I wore braids
freckles and banged-up knees
the Ankle-Grabber stalked my nights.

Faceless creature, he
dwelt in the dust beneath my bed.
His long articulated digits, bone-thin

wrists and arms of palest
green darted out to try to snatch
my legs and ankles as I passed,

to drag me down into ravenous
black. He knew the rules
of our nightly story-- he could not leave

his dusty lair, but only reach
with those hungry arms. If I ran
and leapt from the bedroom door

to swan dive on the spread,
I out-witted him. If I slept centered
in my narrow bed, arms and legs tucked

close beneath the sheets, he
could not reach but gnashed his teeth.
When daylight gleamed across the floor

I leaned over the edge to see--
and found he had transformed
to pooh-poohs blowing about in my breath.

O happy child
whose monsters, obedient to the plot,
turned and vanished in denouement.

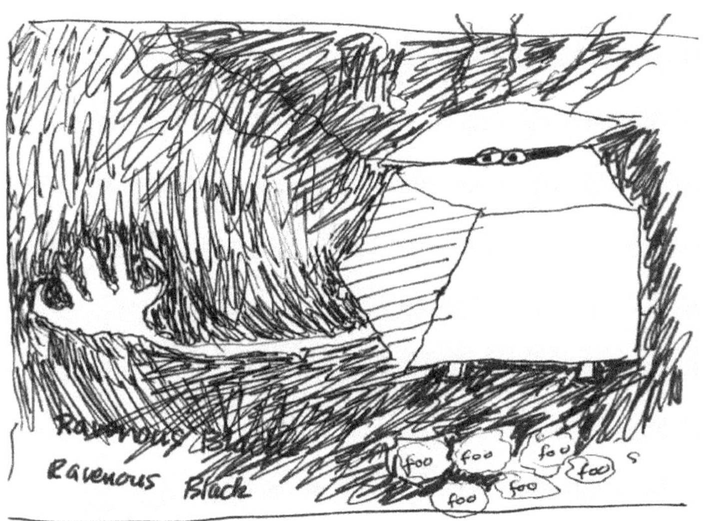

WAFFLES

After my brother was born, we still
squeezed in together on Saturday mornings
around the enamel-topped table, four of us
on red vinyl seats atop sticky chrome legs,
so close our elbows and feet touched.
The baby slept, too small for waffles

Dad manned the waffle iron.
The light winked off, fragrant steam billowed--
"This dark enough for you?"
A chorus of wanting rose. He quartered waffles
with a flick of his musical wrist. Half-way into

my second piece I was painting on extra
butter, watching yellow-melt disappear,
pouring amber into little square pools.
I didn't't hear their words, just the first grating
of sarcasm. I didn't look up until the sharp
crack of my father's palm.
My mother's cheek burned
with a red patch the shape
of father's hand. Her blue
eyes brimmed. She sobbed once,
pushed back her chair. My sister and I
looked at each other. We heard
mother bang her bedroom door.
We looked at our father.
"Eat your waffles," he said.
Our new brother started fussing,
our mother crying.
We looked at our plates and listened.

Finally, he went. Behind their door
we heard their voices.
Eat, I told my sister.
I cut up all the soggy little squares.
And I ate them.

HOLINESS

The summer I turned eleven I sprawled
across my bed as steamy June unwound
reading lives of the saints in heavy books.

Dusty-pink chenille imprinted my pale legs
like St. Rose of Lima's hair-shirt. How
she fought her beauty-- shaved her hair,
roughened her hands with lye soap,
stayed up all night to pray,

knees pressed against cold stone, arms
out-stretched. She snatched my soul
from Therese de Lisieux, that Flower
whose Little Way the sisters recommended.

Finding space for penitence was not easy
in that three-flat stuffed with cousins, sister,
cat, a brother who toddled everywhere.
I chose a narrow spot between the coal bin
and a strip of earth by the wire fence where
Grandpa grew irises and blue morning
glories twisting up.

I told him everything--
my plan to be a Saint, the altar I
would build beside the coal bin door,
how I would kneel on cold cement
my arms out like the cross, perfect
in holy ecstasy. "Humpff" was all he said.

He was pulling out weeds. Humpff.
I made the altar from a box and cloth,
put my statue of the Sacred Heart on top.
Dandelions and daisies withered in a cup.

I sat there with my cat , sometimes said
my rosary too, but ecstasy eluded me.
By twelve I was a sinner.

PIANISSIMO-1

You and I, Sister, in the House of Home

In this house light struck
soundless through dim glass.
sun lay aslant on wooden floors,
dusty parallelograms of such sad gold.
Fading cabbage roses bloomed
soft beneath the tall black piano.
We washed its white keys
as they yellowed slowly.
The licorice bird lay smothered
in its wine velvet nest,
all its colors grown mute.

Sorrow sat dry-eyed in an upholstered chair,
her hands folded in mother's lap.
Turning pages whispered in separate corners.
A clearing throat, soft chimes from the mantel clock,
its every tick. Bafflement stifled our breath,
closed our throats like stone.

Here no one said good-bye. But can't you still hear
the polka's murmur? a faint swirl in the dust?

PIANISSIMO-2

In this house, light struck
soundless through dim glass;
sun lay aslant on the floor, dim
parallelograms of such sad gold.
Cabbage roses bloomed
soft under the tall black piano.
Mother washed its keys
as they yellowed slowly.
All the colors faded.
The licorice clarinet smothered
within its velvet box,
its notes grown mute.

Whispers of turning
pages in separate corners,
a clearing throat, the dark
chime of the mantel clock,
its every tick. No one
said Good-bye.

Can you still hear the polka's
murmur? a faint swirl in the dust?

BETRAYAL

Mother was making soft plashings and swishings
in the tub. I stood outside the closed door
arguing. "Come on in," she called. My hand
paused on the glass knob. "Are you coming in?"

I pushed dark-varnished wood open. Warm, damp
lilac-scented air, white tiles, pink towels with edges
fraying--and my naked mother, a great mound of flesh,
explaining why I couldn't' go to Judy's.
Glistening layers and folds poured off her, filling the whole tub.
I felt my face rearranging itself against my will. "Are you listening?"
With great effort I pulled my gaze upward to meet her
hard eyes. I nodded. "You'd better get out. We'll talk later."

I backed out of the bathroom, closed the door softly. I turned
away. The hall's coolness hit my skin like triumph,
saying, I'll never look like that. I'm better.

BATTLE

We were fighting, sister, then that icicle
hanging near the gate   glinting
in the sun dripping
on your hair

tempted me.

                My mittened hand flew up   grasped its
dagger point   broke off its brittle
gleam and smacked you
on the bean.

Your bellow split
                wide the morning air
your mouth made a blackened hole

but ice gems were bursting in the shine
dancing dazzle round your head
dancing sparkle in my soul.

Ma-a-a-a-a!! you wailed

fleeing toward the house
                leaving me alone
                        with my terrible delight.

Often I have thought of this,
glad I didn't stab instead.

ROAD TRIP LEGENDS

Dad plunged into debt to buy the green Ford
Mom named Leapin' Lizzie, and we escaped
to the campgrounds. Weekends of logistics preceded

each trip as Dad planned necessary miracles
of compression and finesse, then performed them
to fit the gear under, behind, around, on top of us

before we rolled forth from the alley to the Smokies,
Adirondacks, the Rockies or Bust, across America,
a family that worked best in wilderness. My lady

sister slept in goose down on the only cot, grew
hysterical about bugs. Brother shoved bears snout-first
into garbage cans while they fed, hind feet on rim.

In her only Levis ever, Mom climbed switch-backs,
returned to sling slumgullion on the Colman. Dad hurled
rock grenades at the bear clawing our ice chest

while I held the lantern, shaking in midnight's
frigid mountain air and excelled the next day
at boyish bravado and other feats of heartiness.

Breaking camp challenged us. It took half an hour
to collapse the tent and haul everything to the rear
of the car, where Dad was sweating and shoving to repack

as only he could. For two hours, we stood by, alert
as surgical nurses—"Hand me that bag. No, not the duffle,
the tent poles, don't be a ninny." If one of us grew bored,

ventured to place a sleeping bag in the trunk, he erupted—
"That goes on top. Let me do it. How many times
must I tell you?" He needed us to the bitter end,

to help him lash canvas over the heaps of stuff
on the car roof, in the box he designed and built
especially to take us all to the high hills, camping.

Long-Distance Daughter-1

The last time I saw you surely did not count.
From your bedroom door my gaze traveled

such distance to you, propped on pillows,
wearing an oxygen mask, so far away I lost

my breath. This was the day after Tom's wedding,
remaining family clustered around you. It was time

for me to fly from the familiar, complicated
pain of "going home," to return to the family

I was making. I gripped my suitcase, held
my small son by the hand-- the grandson

who would grow-up most like you, his eloquent
fingers finding new music in your old clarinet,

his love of math and swing, the way he tells
funny stories. Balanced on the threshold

of loss, I announced, "Taxi's here. We're leaving."
Did anyone say good-bye? You were struggling

to breathe. I should have known: the long
longing to have you near, the years yearning

for you to see the love you gave me
turned into six lives, generations,

a garden,
a poem without an ending.

April 2021

Long-Distance Daughter-2

When my brother called to tell me your heart stopped,
Dad, I didn't believe. Dinner time, I was clearing,
the main course was over when the phone rang.
Frank answered, murmured, hung up, then came

toward me with his hands out and so much tenderness
in his eyes I started backing away, shaking my head,
No, no. No, he's in the hospital for tests. The floor
opened. Your grandsons, eyes round as plates,

watched their mother fall apart into a chair.
Then she cut their hair, packed, scrubbed floors.
We flew in the morning and were there by lunch.
Later I learned you had been dying for three days,

your heart stopping and starting while I sat on our grass
in late-August sun, writing you a long letter, walked
down the hill to post it. On that day you were fighting
to keep going or to go, I don't know which. After

the funeral I said to my brother, "I'll never understand
why you didn't call me sooner." He looked confused.
"You weren't here," he said. I never asked mother
why she didn't call, but I asked her about the letter.

She never saw it. We don't know where it went.
Years later, near Christmas, I made a small donation
for the Memorial Tree at the mall. On a bit of paper I wrote,
"In Loving Memory of Fletcher Philips." I hung this

in the branches of the memory tree
among small lights and turned to go.
Then--like you—came joy on the wing –
as if you were remembering me.

EXPRESSWAY

The last time I saw my father
he looked so thin and frail he took
my breath from me. In the hotel room
before my brother's wedding, my father

struggled to put on his tux, ruffled shirt,
his vest no bigger than a child's. He sat
on the bed's edge, laughing groom's men
all around, and he gasped and wheezed

pulling on his socks, tying his shiny shoes.
Then the wedding had to wait while he
rested across the rented bed, the flimsy
pink spread, gathering strength for the journey

down the long aisle. My mother's brisk stride
so far outpaced him, he seemed forgotten.
That night, driving home on the Dan Ryan,
my parents huddled in the back of their own

car, while I, their long-distance daughter, gripped
their wheel, speeding in the rain. Shouldn't I
stay in the right lane? Their voices feeble,
their breath mere cobwebs. Mine loud and angry.

Was I frightened? Who did we know who'd died
on the Dan Ryan? I told them to keep quiet.
The wind pushed us, rocking, into the night.
Lights and whizzing spun around us.

PERFECT TESTIMONY- 1

I remember father coming home
every night from at 6:15
as my mother hustled.
At 6:30 sharp we sat for dinner
in the dining room-- white cloth, napkins
folded in silver rings inscribed with our names,
ice-cubes in water crystal. Father turned back his cuffs,
sharpened the carving knife, told jokes from the office,
posed math riddles. We told stories from school.
I remember laughing until my stomach ached.
> *Isn't that strange*, Mother says.
> *Dinner was my worst time.*
> *Everything had to be so perfect..*

PERFECT TESTIMONY- 2

One stifling Chicago summer night
when I was suffering
chicken-pox, I couldn't't sleep.
A utility fixture
on the apartment building
across the alley was casting a glare
onto my pillow and it was too hot
to close the drapes. Father found
an old brush, some left-over black paint
in the basement. He crossed the alley,
entered the building, climbed the stairs, crept
down the hall, removed a screen, leaned far out into the night.
He painted exactly one-half of the offending bulb.
Like magic
light disappeared from my pillow,
light remained for the tenants across the way,
who needed it. I fell asleep encircled
by the shadow my father made.

At the gate of Glenwood School for Boys,
stands a bronze man, his hand on the shoulder
of a homeless and wayward bronze boy:
"A Man is what happens to a Boy" the inscription reads.
I used to think the man was grandfather Philips,
once Headmaster here. His family lived
in the brick house on the Quad where Inez presided
with her silver bell. My father grew up
wearing cadet gray, marching,
studying, playing sax in the band,
pitching sweet-scented Illinois hay.

He started taking me to Old Boys' Day reunions
when I was eight. Hand in hand we toured
buildings and farm, watched precision drills.
Then in chapel my atheist father sang
"A Mighty Fortress Is Our God" with such loud
harmony, people turned to stare. He sang on,
erect, face-front, watery eyes saluting something
I didn't understand. Was it duty?

FIGURING FATHER

The early photos, their sepia-blurred images
glued to black cardboard, corners battered
from seventy years of family use, inspired my mother
to spin stories about her husband's tortured youth.
>   *Look at him!*
She held up "Fletcher at two"
in white dress and stockings, ringlets and sash.
>   *Look how she dressed him. No wonder*
>   *your father has problems.*
Evil Grandmother Inez, who first wore
my nose and reddish hair, reached across the years,
touched me with a crooked finger.
>   *She was cold with her high ideas. Your father visited*
>   *every Sunday, I don't think it was love, really.*
>   *Duty drives your father.*
>   Was it duty made Father care so much
how we sliced the butter?
His fist crashed against the table
rattling dishes, sloshing milk, making
everyone look up, scared and interested.
>   *How many times must I tell you. Don't run your knife*
>   *across the top of the butter?*
His long fingers demonstrated slicing a precise pat.
Did duty make him care about keeping toothpaste tubes
correct?
>   *Someone squeezed the toothpaste in the middle*
>   *last night. Whoever did it should fix it.*
His sloppy family--plump wife with no college degree,
three kids with scabs on their knees and socks falling
into their shoes--must have pained him.

He died young of a failing heart
after yelling at a nurse who woke him in the night
to take his pulse.
My mother told me this is what happened.
I was far away, his long-distance daughter.

  I wish I had been there to hold his hand.

JOURNEY; Spinning Mother's Annual Visit

Roads slick with rain-shine
wound through October trees
and leaf-glow air where leaves exhaled
their last sun-filled dreams in a dimming world,

Mother's yearly visit. Leaf-looking, she called
our silent drives through that gold and crimson
ruin to the inns of our destination. In dark tap rooms
we ordered whiskey sours, on the rocks, and she refilled

our glasses from a flask she kept in a beaded bag
within the womb of her purse, winking at me.
Suddenly loosened, she unpacked her stories,
talking right through anything I said, intent on evolving,

remembering now how her mother dressed her
in starched white ruffles, and her little sister, two dolls
in the soot-covered city. "How could we play? If we touched
a railing, sat on a step, Mother had a fit. It was my fault."

Remembering over and over, year after year,
her earliest perception. She saw herself small, looking up
at her father who chased her giggling mother around the table,
catching her in his arms, their kisses and her own left-out,
lonely feeling.

We almost drew close to each other on those boozy afternoons
while she revised our story in dim, fire-lit rooms,
the autumn drizzle outside and the wet, flaming leaves,
at the center of the glowing, heart-breaking world.

Nov. 19, 2015 (revision of "journey")

THE STORY-WEAVER'S DAUGHTER

Tonight, the moon sails over the house
streaming twisted scarves behind.

Long and billowing, their raveled ends
shine like silver. They are nothing

but windblown vapors, clouds
gilded by the moon's mysterious power.

They remind me of my fabulous mother,
and the stories she told long ago

that trail after me everywhere I go,
dangerous as Isadora's scarves ever were.

Yet I loved listening as she told them,
sitting beside her at the lamp-lit loom.

She wove theories of everyone--
knew how each patterned the fabric

of our family life, why people were
as they were. She wound the warp,

twisted strands of plot around
the pins of her loom, infused

our relatives with colorful strands of failed
convictions, motives black as pitch,

flaws red as the nails she painted
once a year for her husband's

Office Party, where she sat on a hard chair
by the wall, wishing she were home.

Tying-Up Loose Ends

Poems I found scattered in Jane's
computer and file drawers

CONTENTS
Tying Up Loose Ends

The Fight

We bludgeoned each other with words
Until the truth dropped out.
It fell from his mouth,
Clamored into view,
A shinning bell
Of brass

revised
5/9/78

Husband

He is soft and strong.
His hair is stringy on top
And blows about wildly in the wind.
He has long arms to gather me in;
It's warm and safe close to him.
His eyes are sad brown and tired--
I'd give my years to see them shine again.

The one most important thing
I'm making from my life
Is this love with him--
Living-breathing child, woven of tears and bone,
That cries with rapture and pain;
Spirit-skeleton, built of memory and hope,
Which stands when all else is ripped away…

> I gaze at you across the table
> And saw a stranger
> On the other side of a desert
> So, this is "estranged," I thought.
> What a prime word for disemboweling.
> In the Sea -View Motel I vomited my fried clams
> Into a cold white toilet…

But I did eat claims again, just yesterday;
When we loved in the woods
The drab ground was yeasty and the small twigs snapped.

I no longer remember what our long anger was about.
I just remember the vomiting.

C E N T O for the end of summer

breathing
in the night

as sunlight winds back on its dark spool
the stacked, ungraspable shapes of leaves
                              and the grass eking out
                  the last crooked hour of starlight.

or the way the light bends in the trees
this time of year
cold museum light, the brides are breathing in their rooms....

                              so many stars, so bright.

the trees do not know nor the leaves of the grasses hear us:
new green leaves like little licks of fire.
the whole world of the given beating against this garden.

I try to pretend the body's a pod or insect shell
                  and each slow dusk a drawing-down of blinds
                  a single window like a child's nail.
is it the spirit, ransacking through the earth?

the summer night is like a perfection of thought.
a whisper among the viburnums,
                        in the wing-winnowed air:
                  in a world burning up with flowers.

                        ...or was it the perfume
of a woman's hair as she passed below that turned
                over her naked shoulder, down her arm
            and back, the darkness of her hair.

the word *withereth*

        . . . loneliness
squared, raised to the power of color
glows against the growing night.

                        --JM   June 5, 2015

" ……. to say the bitter thing in love's voice."
                              --John Hildebidle

You watched me with strange eyes,
as if seeing for the first time
the daughter you never knew
covering her small son with kisses:
lip-reading his flutter of lashes,
smooth-furred curve of cheek,
sweet stem of neck,
and his intricate ears, warm
like snapdragons in the sun;
brailing the blurred soft shapes of his possibilities
in an ecstasy of kissing.

I looked up and saw you
watching, perceiving
the daughter you never knew with kissing.
Ah, stranger!
Deep, dark
wide, unbridgeable
the chasm your gaze spanned
that day.

                              Mother's Day, 1981
                              J.M.

BUDDHA'S DEATH AT DAZU

Buddha's small disciples, quibbling and scowling, gather
                    around his mammoth reclining form

                that covers the earth like mountains.

They whisper to the curve of his moon crescent mouth.
They murmur in the cave of his ear.

            "Tell us, oh, master. Tell us what to do.

            Which of us should take your place?"

Buddha's breath brushes their cheeks and hair.

It rises
            moves among the leaves of the gingko trees
                            and is gone.

                                —JM

NIGHT MUSE

Sometimes she comes in the night
to stand by my bed. I wake in the imperfect
dark and know she's there, insistent
again--hooves in the grass,
at the curtain's edge star-gleam, seconds falling around a silent rim.
I reach for my pen.

A ghost beauty rises, shape-shifts,
sighs. My fingers will spread
fans of light through the dark. I will rise
dancing, whirl round the room, my husband
sleeps, his heart slow under the blanket mound
breath the rhythm of daffodils' rising through snow
so slowly towards spring.

NOTES--
Soft is the night. I peek round
the wavy edges of the shades to see in the moon's glow
if our deer are there, nibbling bushes again,
their hooves printing the snow with their secret life. . .

The moon's glare--its loud brassy gleam--its sheen on
the face of drifted snow comes in round the shades
brighter than our gray days by far--full of allure--
making me rise to see its glamorous clamor--a still glare.
I open the window in the closet, lean out over the porch

roof, send my steaming breath--luminous clouds from my mouth into the bright air. The snow on the shed--so dry it sifts through my fingers like sparkling sugar. All the trees throw shadows, they branch twice on the snow--double trees--sketches by the moon. . . .So still so perfect this night, sky no darker than a chickadees breast.

FLESH

Now you see those two
the white mother drawn and furrowed

the marble folds of her gown breaking
around the ledges of her grief

her knees spread wide to receive him back.
Across her lap he lays waste

pale as a plowed field of chalk. You would think
he would run through her fingers.

Mix the seeds with a cup of sand
scatter them across the prepared ground

water with tears and watch.
You will see the nub--the pain-filled point

where growth erupts
feeling for the light.

It does not look back.
It forgets the ground.

      --Jane Meneghini

On a paper draft of this poem, I found this following last citation;
[3/9/24]   Torn by the plow
       Over and over again

Botticelli's "Birth of Venus" ca--1486

It's not as if I didn't know you.
Cliche of a hundred art books,
over-exposed deity riding
shoreward on your half-shell,
paged by with a yawn. Yet here
amid the gallery-hum, the shuffle
of sneakers, a museum headache
coming on, my small sons tugging
the hem of my jacket, the din
of the ordinary everywhere--here

you strike me to stillness and don't let me go.

Like the attendant Hour
on the windy shore, dress billowing
who reaches out, eager to enwrap
your famous body in a rosy cloak,

I too am lifted off my feet by the force of your arrival.

Like Zephyrus and the nymph at his side
who lean toward you, lean on the air,
he red-faced from puffing the ruffling waves,
she exhaling a shower of tumbling flowers--

I too lean toward you who have taken my breath.

Newborn whole from the sea, larger than life,
still center of motion and effort around you,
what witchery carries you over that ancient sea
to meet me here on this alien shore, grasp my soul

and wrench awe from the core of my skeptical being?

Big as life she moves toward you riding a giant scallop
shell like a surf board.
New-born from the sea and glowing with life, her flesh
lit from within
Though about to step ashore, she gives the impression
of an absolute stillness. (radiant and still as a pearl.

Around Venus all is effort and motion.
ON the left, winged Zephyrus and Aura lean toward her
from the air blowing mightily;
their wind-breath releases a tumble of small pink
flowers and gently ruffles the sea, moving the shell
forward. On the right an attendant floating just above
the shore leans into the gale
as she holds out a large, rose-colored garment, ready to

wrap it around Venus like a cape. The attendant's light, blossom trimmed gown, her hair, and the cape all ripple in the wind.

The tall, lean figure of Venus remains still, only a few locks of her knee-length blonde hair ruffled by the wind. Her left hand, fingers splayed, covers one breast and her heart, her right hand holds the bottom of her hair to cover her genitals. Her light hazel eyes, her face, her motionless pose are serene. She stands before you in the fullness of her power to wrench awe from the core of your being.

--Jane Meneghini

Squeezed: or, Down-sizing

Late afternoon [Feb. 2, 2015]
feeling of fullness
warmth in winter
a goldening
Something in the slant-light
a glow, a slow
lingering warmth
across the snow.
Shadows long and slant
and blue
but warm around
the edges like
a spotlight. [??]

Where does the dark begin?

If we knew it would come to this
could we have altered it?
Made change, given change
a chance?
Along the shore, the land
ravels into strands
The sound of [stones] rattling
sound of the strand
the long retreating roar
heard [by Arnold in "Dover Beach"]
        shingles, shingles.
And off Bar Harbor the essence
of the round stones
So perfect in form
so teasing, so from somewhere
else. Where were they when I was small
a speck of life in my mother?
They were there—foundational.

The foundation ravels out in shingles.
What does it mean, this groping
toward some round meaning . . . [
How we stumble, looking for
candles in the dark.
How much we see, we behold
in a single, wavering flame.

JM June 2018

<u>**The War**</u>

I remember Stuka dive-bombers whizzing at me
                              from the newsreel.

I remember watching with approving sadness
              Hitler sending 15 year-old German boys
                              against Russians.

I remember the dark drone overhead
              of bombers dropping leaflets on blacked-out
                              Chicago practicing.

I remember the cold wind blowing as I walked for the streetcar
              wool sweater, wool skirt, wool hat and jacket--my bare
                      legs freezing-no nylons because of the war.

I remember the iodine smell, rows of cots, stacks of bandages
                  in the basement of Butchie Beaton's building.

I remember gold stars dangling from the window shades along
                  the alley of the street where I lived.

I remember seeing the stars, shinning on them
                  made them so bright
I remember in the evening, in the dark even the moon
                  made them a sight.

I remember newspaper maps of Nazi-Fascist
                  advance and retreat.

I remember hugging brown paper bags full of flattened tin
cans, heading for scrap-metal mountain, empty-lot
the war on Colfax Ave.

I remember Okinawa---the smell of mingled steel and blood.

Journal Entry for Refugees, March 2017

A long night of moonlight
lambent on field and road
dyeing the banks of jumbled snow blue
the tree outside my window
flinging its branching river of limbs
aslant across the yard, its long
trunk of emphatic double-blue. . .

All made of memory tonight
and the longing for a tree
after today's desert of devotion
to the screen on my desk, the brightly lit
closeness of refugees, their confounding
needs and losses. Imagine. To be bereft of all
possibility, all order, all power and citizenship.
Torn from the familiar
branches of family and friends. Riven
from the structures that made life possible
from the roots and walls and roofs of home.
Blown across continents like leaves
having only the colors you and your children wear
and whatever hope and optimism
you remember having once had
when the true meaning of your life
filled you like a great tree.

--Jane Meneghini, Nov. 2017

Poem for Victoria

I had a grand-daughter named for joy.
Here is her face that was
Bright as a gold leaf falling singly down

To the chilled earth closing.
She was warm as blossoms, her skin out-shone
the new-made frost.

Ask not why
the grass stays green. The garden is cut down.
Crickets shake in the shrubs,

Their cries grown feeble beneath cold rocks.
The trees are all unravelling.
Sharp wind gnaws the empty room.

I had a grand-daughter
Bright as all my summers, golden
as the leaf-strewn ground.

GUILT

1.

One summer morning Cheryl found fifty dollars
inside her saddle shoe
left perhaps by a man visiting her parents
she said.

A mystery man as vague and dark
as Brenda Star's.

Cheryl didn't tell her parents.
"Let's go to Cunis's for ice cream"
she said.

We met there twice a day
for weeks
devouring every sundae and soda,
slurping every malted on the menu,
before settling on our favorites.

Meanwhile we discussed
Cheryl's strange benefactor.

From all this excess
Cheryl grew breasts.

2.
Because I walked along the grass
between the married student apartments
instead of on the sidewalk
I saw her through her kitchen window
not more than two yards away.
Her startled gaze leaped
from the page of the book
propped on the coffee pot.
Her spoon stopped
half-way between the bowl of ice cream
and her open mouth.
Guilt fell over her face
the way venetian blinds open
and I couldn't look away.

3.
Five cub scouts waiting for cones
shamble against each other
sneakers scuffing the little white tiles
fingers printing the glass.

Their blue-eyed den mother,
her red hair a frizzled halo,
chats and laughs with the girl
who digs deep into the Rocky Road

while wisps of vapor
rise around her like clouds.
The air is filled with the scent
of frozen cream and sugar and chocolate.

Suddenly the floor seems to open
under my feet and I sink
remembering that I have no place,
no more place, among these innocents.

--Jane Meneghini

Hagar in the Wilderness

Fleeing blows and taunts from her mistress
Hagar stumbles unseeing through burning sand
until she comes on the well in the wilderness,

that green place. There she hauls up a bucket,
sinks to her knees and drinks its bright drops--
water brimming cool and sweet as her thought

of Abraham. The child in her womb trembles.
Hagar lies beneath the palms, hearing her heart's
wild beating. The desert wind stirs and breathes
in the fronds, and a voice is calling her name:
"Hagar, oh, Hagar, full of fear and alone..."
Is it the wind that sees her? or Abraham--?

"El Roi--Who Sees Me--" she answers. Only the wind
touches her hair, murmuring. "Hagar, return
to Sarah's tent. Live, for your child

will pour forth a nation." When the sun bleeds
crimson into the sand and the wind is a hand
pushing her back, Haggar turns toward the east

where her mistress, bitter as drought, waits.
Haggar, mother of mothers without comfort, gathers
        her robes. She returns, carrying hope to a barren
place.

Harrisville Seasons

Good Friday: First Afternoon of Spring (2008)

Like the Arctic   the wind
whistles over the glassy
snow   the dazzling sun

ice mountains of mutant snow
crowd the door way
bury the shrubs   cancel the garden

no ground   but down
on the roads   cold corduroy
frozen in brown ruts

Christmas wreath
still hanging
its red ribbon trailing off like a scrawl of good intentions

April Afternoon

Next to the pile of old snow
where the dog sprawls snoozing
her rake uncovers, under leafmold,
a single purple crocus almost blooming.

July Afternoon

She is tying the delphiniums' tall blue
to slender stakes of green bamboo
deep in flowers when humming

bird appears beside her ear
fanning her cheek with breath
of his wings blurring and whirring
figments dimming the sunny air
carrying him up, down, sideways, reverse
darting, pausing, sorting purple
petals and blue, dipping, sipping
        among black and white frills
oh finding honey   while she
stands transfixed, struck still by his spell
        with twine in her hands
beyond words, past thought
but for that bit of voice in her brain
that says, *look, look,* oh *see*
the *emerald,* or is it *olive,*
the *glint of his back, all the greens
of the woods, shifting,* and *the throb
of the shine of his ruby red throat.*

Harrisville Thawing

From ice-brimmed Nubanusit the water comes
slipping through wetlands in Mosquito Bush
where a redwing calls from a hollow stem.
Towards Harrisville Pond the waters push

slipping through wetlands and Mosquito Bush
east of Biddewee, south out of Child's Bog.
Into Mill Village waters merge and rush
in brick-lined channels and over stones and logs,

east of Biddewee and south out of Child's Bog.
Water tumbles through town, it spills and roars
through narrow brick and stone, over small dams;
under the boiler house, under the Mills it pours.

It tumbles through town, through spillways roars
entering steel turbines that time has stilled.
Under the Boiler House and Granit Mill it pours.
The cascade foams and claws the air as it falls

to enter steel turbines that time has stilled.
Beyond Granite Mill the water flows free.
It foams and roars at the air; then grows still;
slows and widens through wetland reeds.

Beyond the mills where the stream drifts free
wandering hummocks of winter-browned grass
and dark water spreads through broken reeds,
a woman stands watching an otter swim past.

Leaving the hummocks of winter-bent grass,
the stream runs strong under Hancock Road.
The season's first otter swims by and past
into Skatutakee, snow-pale, darkwater-edged.

Dark water streams under Hancock Road
through a stand of trees clutching ice-humped muds
In snow-pale Skatutakee, darkwater-edged,
a stranded fishing shack tilts in slush.

Tree roots clutch the mud-rimmed shore.
Lake water flows under snow and ice
and under the fishing shack tilting in slush.
Rills are singing down the lakeside hills.

The woman stands on the bridge and listens.
Red-wings call from stem to stem.
The stream runs dark in the morning sun.
From ice-brimmed Nubanusit the water comes.

--jane meneghini, Jan. '08 / March 2019

Note: A pantoum is a verse form that repeats lines and sounds
in an intricate pattern that creates an obsessive, hypnotic effect.
It seemed this form just might be able to capture a Harrisville thaw.

Nightwork Revision, 3/14/03

outside the house the moon
round as a spotlight
searches the apple tree
where a tire
hangs on a frozen rope
its blue-shadow double
falling
across bright snow

a dream girl
hangs from blue
velvet ropes far above
pale faces strung in rows
like beads
the circle
of brilliance fastens her
she thinks
she feels the thousand eyes
of strangers holding her
heat of held breaths
tumble of hearts
in the humming darkness
of their fascination
only these seem real
and the searing light
the pitch of the trapeze as she leaps--

she does not believe
the possible plunge
to oblivion

the sleeper
turns toward the light
at the window
sighs in the airy space
where all things are suspended
then cries out

-Jane Meneghini

Litany for Diana

Supermarket Tabloid Headline, 1999: "Why She Died"

shy Di, they called you. from the beginning
your name said mortality. no one noticed.

virginal as Diana   captured   to mother kings
ink-smudged breeder of headlines

medium for the media, your substance spun
to hype, you grew wan as a spider web.

wafer thin, your bones wrapped
in English cloth draped, swathed, hemmed

patroness of the paparazzi
queen of the honey-weavers 'hive,

a goddess in a big blue hat,   bending
over someone small   and sick.

now they keep printing and printing your face
on dolls, on stamps, on collector's plates.

you fail to resurrect.

your story's unraveled
like a comet's tail

with a dark prince you entered
a black hole in the city of light

and disappeared

--Jane Meneghini

String Theory at Night

Oh blue wind falling around the house.
Blaze of moon running along the eaves
to be dashed against stones. Lost
under down and sheets a woman dreams
red beetles are crawling in the lilies,

wakes to feel her heart walking
through her body. The universe times
its blizzard of vibrating strings
like musical rubber bands
so small their existence can't be known.
Meanwhile New Zealand issues a flatulence tax
on sheep and cows
to fight global warming.
Heaviness dimples the fabric of space and time.

She runs pregnant through the woods.
The last cave collapses. Sky explodes
In Sunflowers.

JM April 2009